Contents

What are crocodiles and alligators?

Alligators, crocodiles, caiman and gavials are all crocodilians. They are reptiles that live in water and are related to lizards, snakes, tortoises and turtles. Crocodilians were alive when dinosaurs walked the Earth. Today there are about 23 different species.

Are lizards crocodilians?

Gecko

Lizards are reptiles but are not crocodilians. They have a different type of skull and heart as well as other parts.

No, lizards are not crocodilians.

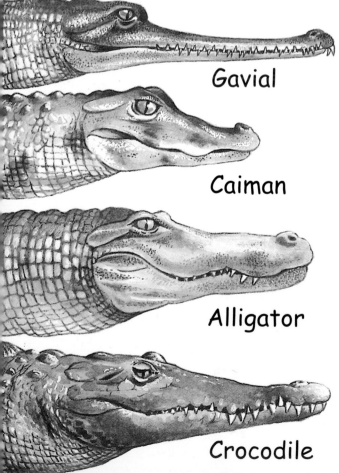

Gavial

Caiman

Alligator

Crocodile

It can be difficult to tell the difference between types of crocodilians. When a crocodile's mouth is closed some of its teeth slide into a C-shaped groove on either side of the top jaw. The teeth can be seen when the mouth is closed. Alligators and caiman don't have these grooves so the teeth in the same position cannot be seen when their mouths are fully closed.

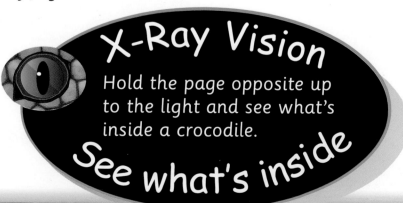

X-Ray Vision

Hold the page opposite up to the light and see what's inside a crocodile.

See what's inside

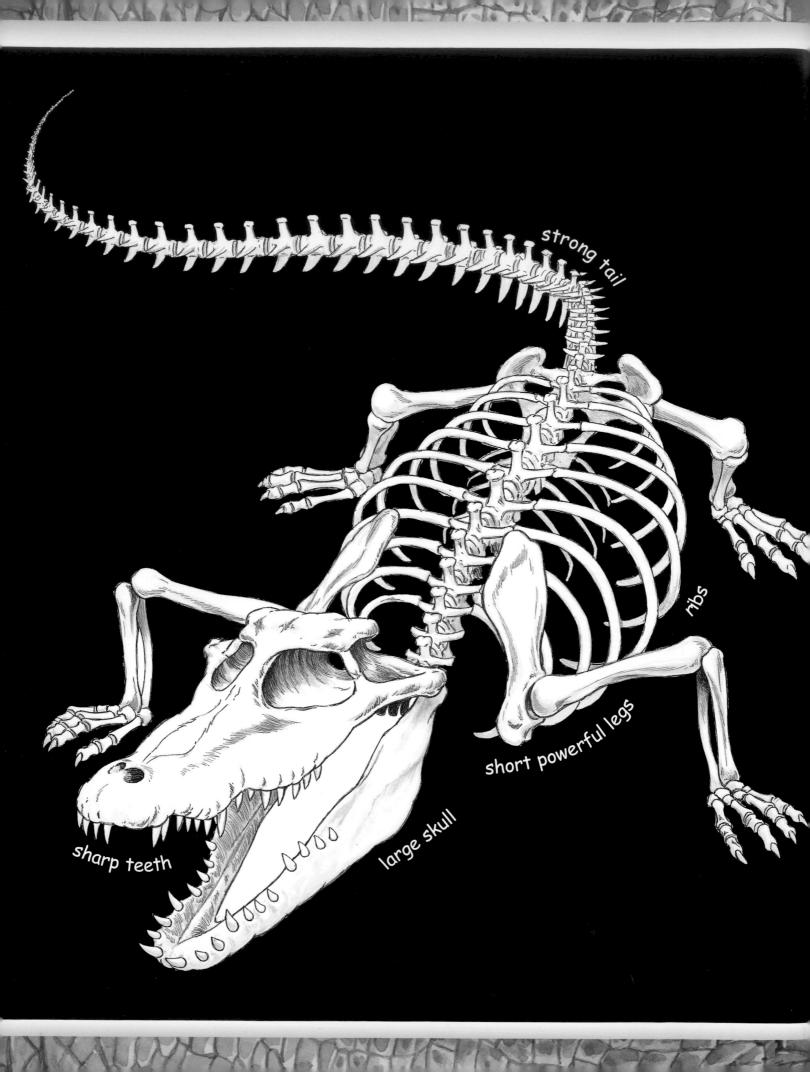

What's inside a crocodilian?

Crocodilians are designed for living in water. The skeleton is long and flexible, making it streamlined. The eyes and nostrils are high up on the long, pointed skull, letting the animal see and breathe even when the rest of its body is submerged. A powerful muscular tail propels crocodilians through the water when swimming.

Did you know?

Crocodiles can replace their teeth. When an old tooth is lost, a new one grows from below to replace it. A 4-metre-long Nile crocodile would have gone through more than 45 sets of teeth!

old tooth

new tooth

Cutaway of a crocodile to show its organs

The lower chamber of the heart is almost completely divided into two halves. This makes a crocodilian's blood circulation far more efficient than in other reptiles.

lungs

intestines

heart

liver

stomach

webbed toes

nostrils

crocodile's upper jaw

A good sense of smell helps crocodilians find prey hidden in murky water. They also have sense organs, on scales along the sides of the jaws, that help with this.

How do crocodilians see, hear and smell?

Most crocodilians' are nocturnal and their eyes are designed to help them hunt at night. A slit-like vertical pupil lets more light in and a mirror-like layer at the back of the eye shines light back on to the retina. With binocular vision they can also judge distances – very important for a predator.

Crocodile on a river bank, watching for prey

Alligator swimming partly submerged

A special see-through eyelid
protects a crocodilian's eyes
when the animal is underwater.

Did you know?

Crocodiles have good
hearing. Flaps cover the
ear openings to protect
the ears when a
crocodile is underwater.

A crocodile floating almost submerged (left) can leap out of the water in a flash to catch a bird flying over a metre above it.

How do crocodilians move?

On land, crocodilians crawl on their stomach or lift it off the ground and do the 'high walk', dragging their tail behind them. If alarmed, they walk then slide down a slope into the water. Crocodilians can also gallop. They lift their body off the ground and they sweep their tail from side to side.

Did you know?

At night, a Nile crocodile can travel a distance of 10 km across land.

Crocodilians tuck their front legs into the sides of their body when swimming. They use their tail to propel themselves through the water (right).

Crocodilians are amphibious. In water they are excellent swimmers, using their powerful tail to speed them along. The tail sweeps from side to side in a rippling s-shaped pattern. Many crocodilians have webbed feet but their legs are usually held close to the body and are not used when swimming.

With its stomach touching the ground, a crocodilian slowly crawls along. They can speed up to a gallop, reaching about 18 kph (below).

Where do crocodilians live?

Crocodilians can only live in tropical and subtropical areas. As they are cold-blooded, they need to bask in the sun to warm up. They live close to water where they have a ready supply of food. They can live in large rivers or small streams, marshes, swamps, ponds, creeks and by the sea. Crocodiles cool off by submerging in water.

Did you know?

The small reservoir at Sierra Leone University was home to several West African dwarf crocodiles – until some of the gardeners caught and ate them!

12 Saltwater, or estuarine, crocodile basking

Did you know?

At cool and dry times of the year crocodilians often hide away in burrows or in quiet ponds and don't eat. They wait there until the weather gets better.

Saltwater crocodile on a river bed

What do crocodilians eat?

Crocodilians are carnivores. Small crocodilians or young eat insects, crayfish, crabs, frogs and small fish. As they grow bigger they can catch larger prey, including small mammals, lizards, snakes, turtles and birds. Very big crocodilians will even catch wildebeest, zebras, monkeys, deer and people. Crocodilians don't always catch live prey – they will happily eat carrion.

14 Nile crocodiles eating a zebra

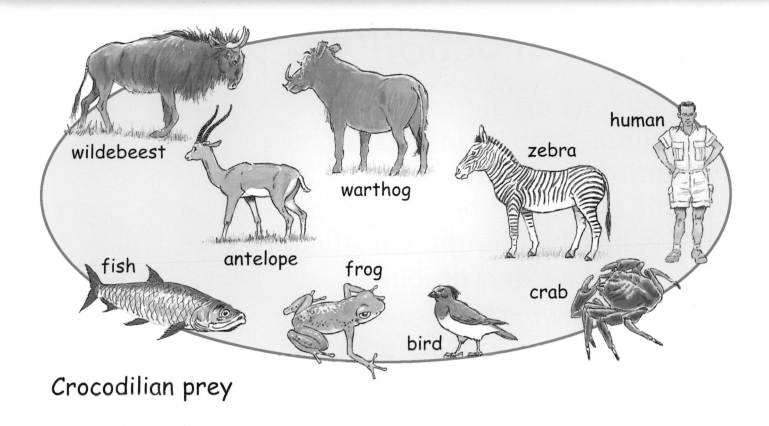

Crocodilian prey

Crocodilians don't need to eat very often. One alligator was known to survive 1,591 days without eating. A large crocodilian will usually feast once a week. It then takes several days for the meal to be digested.

Odd things have been found inside alligators' and crocodiles' stomachs, including vehicle number plates, spears, kettles, bullets and food cans.

Did you know?

The Cuban crocodile can snatch perching birds from the branches of trees overhanging rivers.

How do crocodilians hunt?

Crocodilians are fierce hunters. Hatchlings snap at insects, small fish and frogs. Older animals lie in wait and stalk their prey. Large prey is grabbed by the crocodilian's powerful jaws and dragged underwater where it drowns. The crocodilian grips its prey hard and spins it fast. This will make sure the prey is dead and helps to rip the prey to pieces.

Many crocodilians eat stones (above). They help to grind up food in the stomach and are called gastroliths.

Many crocodilians store their dead prey underwater where it rots and becomes tender to eat.

Did you know?

A crocodile can slam its jaws shut with a force of 13 tonnes. This can easily smash the leg of a cow or crush a turtle.

Saltwater crocodile

Do crocodilians lay eggs?

Male and female crocodilians mate underwater. A few weeks later, the female makes a nest at night. This can be a hole dug in the ground or a mound of earth or vegetation. The eggs are kept warm by the sun or by the heat given off from rotting plants.

Female crocodilians guard their nest. When the eggs hatch, she carefully carries the young to the water for safety.

Depending on the age and species of crocodilian, between 10 and 60 eggs are laid (left). They hatch between 50 and 115 days later.

X-Ray Vision

Hold the page opposite up to the light and see what's inside crocodile eggs.

See what's inside

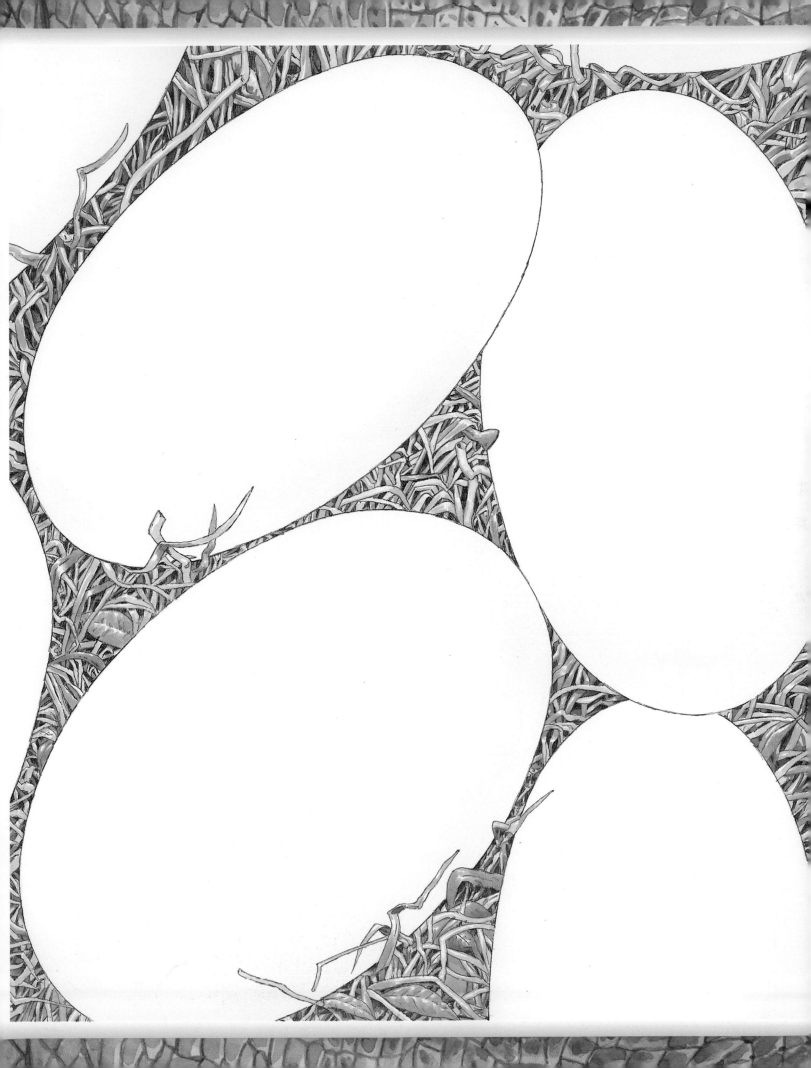

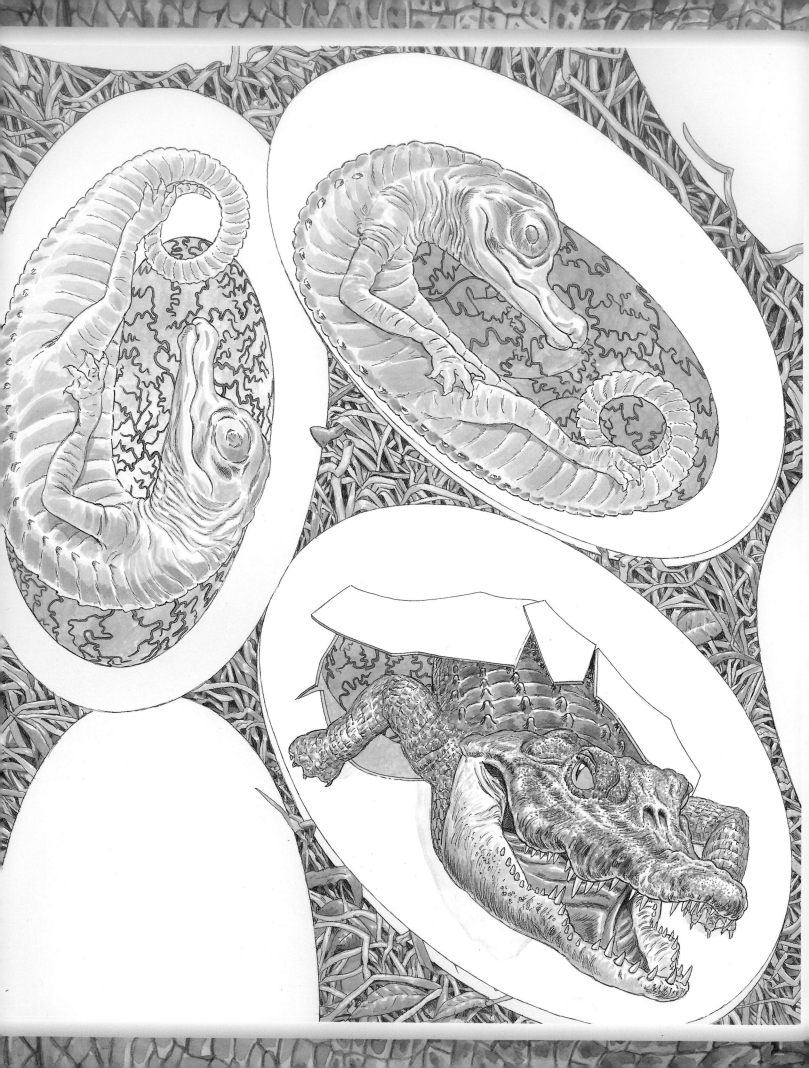

Do crocodilians have enemies?

Except for humans, few animals will attack an adult crocodilian. Jaguars are known to attack nesting females. If a crocodile gets in the way of an elephant, lion, hippopotamus or rhinoceros it might be attacked. Some large snakes, such as the anaconda, will feed on crocodilians. Crocodilian eggs are eaten by monitor lizards and the hatchlings are at risk from birds such as the marabou stork.

Crocodilians will sometimes fight each other (right) and younger animals will kill and eat each other.

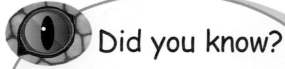 Did you know?

If baby crocodiles are in danger their mother may pick them up and keep them in her mouth pouch for safety.

21

Why do people kill crocodilians?

It is hard for crocodilians to live near humans. People are frightened of them and will kill them because several species of crocodilian attack people. Around 2,000 people each year are killed by alligators and crocodiles. But most crocodilians keep away from humans and are harmless.

Did you know?

Crocodilians are also hunted for their skins. Each year thousands of illegal stuffed crocodilians, skins and other products are confiscated by government officials throughout the world.

Confiscated caiman skins in South America

Crocodilian skin is made into bags, shoes, wallets, clothes and belts. But there is no need to kill crocodilians when other materials can be made to look just like it (above).

Did you know?

Many crocodilians are protected under international law, including the black caiman and the American crocodile. Some species are now farmed for their skins. Any skin or object made from a crocodilian and sold today must have a certificate to prove it has not been taken from a wild animal.

In tropical and subtropical areas, tourists may find all kinds of things for sale made from illegally killed crocodilians, such as this hideous pen holder (below).

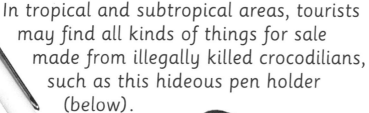

Confiscated pen holder with an illegal stuffed crocodile head

Crocodilian stories and legends

Their large size and fierce nature means that crocodilians have become part of the folklore of many cultures. They have been worshipped as gods and linked with the origins of mankind. They have also been the source of some dragon legends. In the past, crocodilians were often feared and killed as evil monsters.

Sebek

In ancient Egypt, crocodiles were honoured and kept in ponds. The larger ones had their foreheads decorated. The Egyptians worshipped a crocodile-headed god called Sebek (right) who was believed to carry dead kings to the underworld.

Aboriginal image of a crocodile

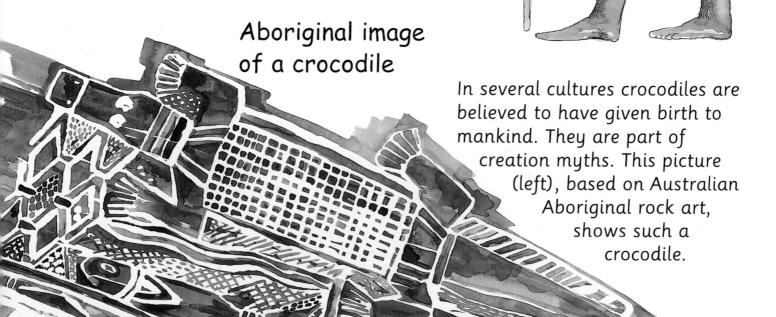

In several cultures crocodiles are believed to have given birth to mankind. They are part of creation myths. This picture (left), based on Australian Aboriginal rock art, shows such a crocodile.

The stories of European dragons in the Middle Ages told of fire-breathing, people-eating monsters. These fierce dragons were feared because they brought disaster and death. Some pictures of them (right) are believed to be based on Nile crocodiles.

European image of a dragon

Chinese dragons seem to be made up of parts of crocodilians and cobra snakes. These wise and powerful dragons are important in Chinese mythology. They were often shown on Chinese pottery, clothes and ornaments like this vase (below).

In parts of Africa, keeping crocodile teeth is believed to protect against crocodile attacks, lightning, evil spirits and illness, and also to bring good luck.

How old are crocodilians?

Crocodiles are the closest living relatives of the extinct dinosaurs which roamed Earth over 200 million years ago.

One hundred and ten million years ago there were dinosaur-eating monster crocodiles. Remains of the super-crocodile Sarcosuchus (right) were discovered in 1997 in the Sahara Desert. The teeth of another, called Deinosuchus, were found in 1858. Deinosuchus roamed North America from New Jersey to Montana.

Protosuchus (left) lived over 200 million years ago, in North America. This one-metre-long hunter had dagger-like teeth and was a fast runner and swimmer. Protosuchus was another ancestor of today's crocodilians.

Protosuchus

Stenosaurus fossils

Did you know?

The oldest known crocodile died in 1997 in a Russian zoo, aged 115. Nile crocodiles can live to 45 in the wild and up to 80 years in captivity.

Stenosaurus is an ancestor of the gavial. Stenosaurus lived 200-145 million years ago.

Sarcosuchus

Sarcosuchus (above) was a giant animal, the length of a bus. At 50-60 years old it reached its full size of 11-12 m and weighed 8 tonnes.

27

Crocodilians around the world

Crocodilians live in the tropics and subtropics of the world – the areas around the Equator where it is always hot.

American alligator

American alligators like swamps and marshes, but also live in rivers, lakes and ponds in south-eastern USA.

Cuvier's dwarf caiman

Cuvier's dwarf caiman is the smallest crocodilian. It lives in the forest rivers of tropical South America.

The common caiman is found in Central and South America, Mexico, the USA, the West Indies, Cuba and Puerto Rico.

Common caiman

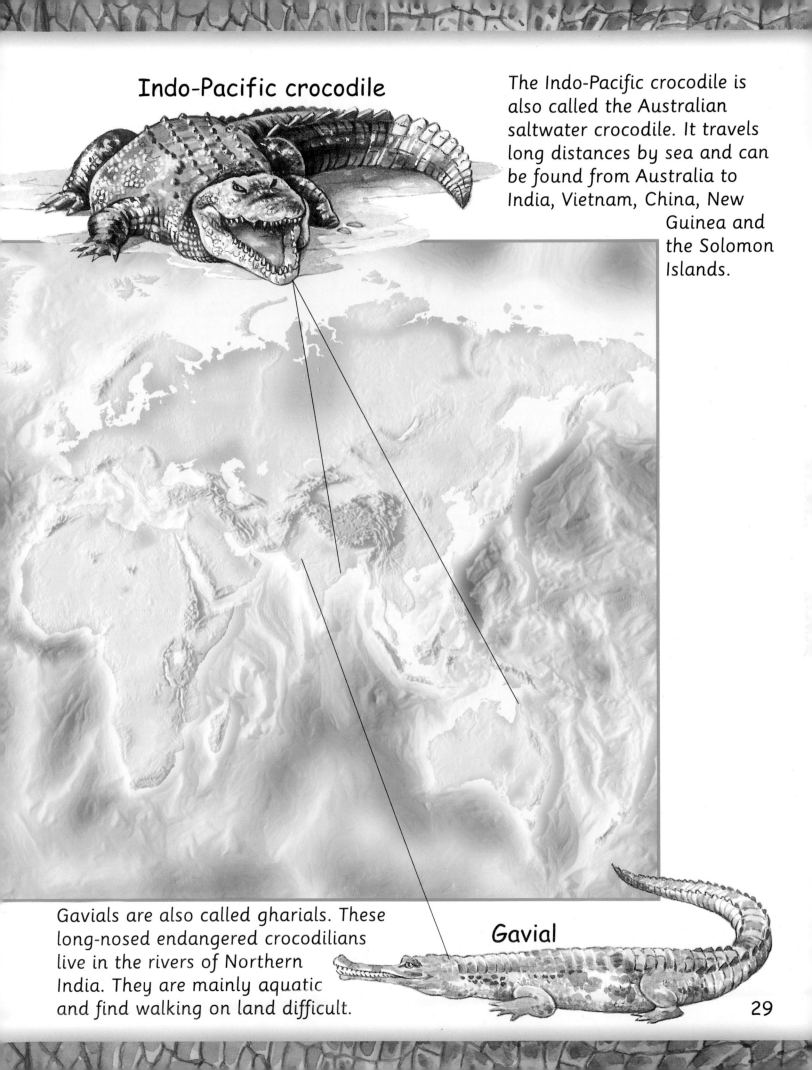

Indo-Pacific crocodile

The Indo-Pacific crocodile is also called the Australian saltwater crocodile. It travels long distances by sea and can be found from Australia to India, Vietnam, China, New Guinea and the Solomon Islands.

Gavials are also called gharials. These long-nosed endangered crocodilians live in the rivers of Northern India. They are mainly aquatic and find walking on land difficult.

Gavial

Crocodilian facts

When fish are migrating crocodiles work together to catch them. They form a semi-circle across the river and herd the fish into a group. Then they eat the fish closest to them.

Nile crocodiles live throughout much of Africa. They are not fussy about where they live and can be found in lakes, rivers and swamps.

Cuban crocodiles are only found in the Lanier and Zapata swamps of Cuba and are now endangered.

The rounded end of the gavial's snout is probably used to make sounds during mating.

The saltwater crocodile is the largest living species, reaching over 9 m in length.

An adult male alligator will bellow out a warning if it hears a car horn or similar noise. The sound makes the animal think there is a rival in its territory.

The word alligator comes from the Spanish 'el lagarto' meaning 'the lizard'. Caiman is a Spanish word for any type of crocodilian.

Nile crocodiles are the most common predator in Africa. One hundred years ago, about 3,000 people were killed by these crocodiles each year.

More than 40 people were eaten by saltwater crocodiles when a boat sank in a river in the Celebes, Indonesia.

To pretend to be sad can be called 'crocodile tears'. In fact, crocodiles cannot cry but the shiny skin around their eyes can look like tears.

One Nile crocodile was found to have tried to swallow too big a meal – it died with a turtle stuck in its throat.

In 1944, saltwater crocodiles were thought to have killed hundreds of Japanese soldiers overnight.

Glossary

amphibious To live both in water and on land.

binocular vision The ability to see the same area with both eyes at the same time.

captivity To be kept in a man-made environment, such as a zoo.

carnivore Any animal that eats the flesh of other animals as its main food.

carrion Dead animals and decaying flesh.

confiscate To take banned items away from someone.

digest To pass food through the body.

endangered Animals that are few in numbers and may be close to extinction.

extinct Species of animals that are no longer alive anywhere in the world.

hatchlings Young just hatched from their eggs.

migrating The movement of animals from one place to another to find food or better conditions.

nocturnal An animal that is active at night.

predator Any animal that hunts other living creatures for food.

prey Any animal that is hunted by other animals for food.

pupil The opening in the eye where light passes through to the retina.

retina The part of the eye at the back that is sensitive to light. The retina sends the sensation of vision to the brain.

species A group of living things that look alike, behave in the same way and can interbreed.

stalking To creep up on prey quietly and unseen.

streamlined Made to move through air or water more easily.

submerge To sink or dive below the water's surface.

subtropical Areas of the world that are just outside the tropics but still have a hot climate.

tropical The area of the world near the Equator, where it is always hot.

Index